Original title:
Rhymes of Relativity

Copyright © 2025 Creative Arts Management OÜ
All rights reserved.

Author: Lorenzo Barrett
ISBN HARDBACK: 978-1-80567-840-3
ISBN PAPERBACK: 978-1-80567-961-5

Temporal Tides

Time wobbles like a jelly,
A clock that's gone astray,
Seconds dance in silly patterns,
Ticking in a playful way.

Past and future swap their hats,
What's now may soon be then,
The moment slips and slides around,
Like children dodging their den.

Yesterday wore polka dots,
Tomorrow's dressed in stripes,
Today just giggles in the mirror,
With chocolate cream delights.

Compression here, expansion there,
A rubber band of lore,
In this crazy cosmic spin,
Who knows what's in store?

Flight of the Fantastical

Flying pigs play chess up high,
With lizards on a spree,
While unicorns in shades of blue,
Sip tea beneath a tree.

Balloons that talk and giggle loud,
Sail past the stars, oh joy!
On moonbeams made of marshmallow,
With laughter to deploy.

Ducks in spacesuits do the twist,
In dances smooth and grand,
They twirl through cosmic kitchens,
With hamster chefs on hand.

Believe in all the wild and weird,
For magic soars above,
In flights of pure imagination,
That sprinkle dreams with love.

Space Between the Lines

In margins small, where words collide,
A joke sits waiting still,
A wink from every letter finds,
A chuckle on the hill.

Commas giggle, semicolons grin,
As sentences chase their tails,
Between the lines of scribbled notes,
Are tiny cosmic trails.

In every parentheses, joy hides,
A riddle wrapped in cheer,
Reading sideways, looking up,
The fun is always near.

So take a peek and read between,
For laughter's what we seek,
These funny thoughts in written form,
Are treasures that we speak.

Wavelengths of Wonder

Waves of giggles bounce and roll,
Like jellybeans in flight,
In a spectrum of absurdity,
Colors shining bright.

Frequencies of silly sounds,
Dance on air like sprites,
Tuning in to chuckles,
In laughter's sweet delights.

The spectrum spins, and oh my stars,
What wonders do arise,
From wavelengths that can twist and turn,
Like carrots in disguise.

So tune your ears to laughter's wave,
And let your spirits soar,
In wavelengths of unbounded joy,
There's always room for more!

Sonnet of the Stars

In the cosmos where oddities play,
Stars twinkle like lights on a Broadway.
Planets wobble, they dance out of tune,
Making jests of the afternoon.

Gravity's a joke that makes us all fall,
While comets gossip in a celestial hall.
Black holes chuckle, they swallow with glee,
As we spin around like a dizzy bee.

Universal Sonance

In the void where echoes collide,
A sound so silly, we try to hide.
Galaxies giggle, in spirals they swirl,
While quasars twang like a cosmic girl.

We strut with aliens, with two left feet,
In a dance-off with gravity, oh what a feat!
The Milky Way's chuckle, a shimmering sight,
As we trip through the cosmos, all merry and bright.

Flowing Through the Void

Drifting through space on a wave of good cheer,
Asteroids throwing a celestial beer.
Cosmic confetti, it floats all around,
In the grand parade where no one is found.

Meteor showers rain down like balloons,
As we sing silly space-time tunes.
The universe laughs with a twinkle and wink,
Oh, what a ride on this interstellar link!

Harmonies of the Hereafter

Afterlife jokes from a celestial stand,
Spirits stuff marshmallows, life unplanned.
Galactic giggles echo in strife,
Tickling stardust to encourage life.

In the afterglow, we wear hats that align,
With echoes of laughter that dance through time.
On a blanket of cosmos, we sing absurd,
In the strange loops of space, we've always heard!

Looping Starlight

Up in the cosmos, stars take a dance,
They twirl and they spin, giving time a chance.
A comet slips by, it winks with a tease,
While Saturn's rings play hopscotch with ease.

Galaxies giggle, they stretch and they yawn,
A black hole grins, like a mischievous fawn.
Light years explode in a cosmic balloon,
As planets parade, a bizarre cartoon.

Space Between the Notes

In the concert of space, planets hum low,
Singing sweet tunes like a cosmic radio.
The comets join in with their tail of bright spark,
Making sound waves bounce on the edges of dark.

Between every note, there's a giggle or sigh,
A wink from a meteor zooming on by.
The universe sways in a whimsical way,
As rhythm and chaos enjoy their ballet.

Frequencies of Being

Vibrations of laughter ripple through time,
As waves of existence play peek-a-boo rhyme.
In this funky dimension, we dance with our feet,
To the beat of the atoms that can't keep a seat.

Bubbles of laughter float high in the air,
While gravity chuckles, no worries, no care.
Dancing on quarks, we spin like a top,
In a universe giggling, we never will stop.

Veils of Infinity

Behind every star, there's a joke waiting round,
Wrapped in a veil, where the giggles abound.
The space-time continuum thinks it's so sly,
While we trace its pathways and laugh as we fly.

Infinity's layers peel back just for laughs,
Revealing a world full of whimsical daffs.
As we tumble through realms where the punsters decide,
The cosmos, a playground, where humor's our guide.

Frames of Reality

In a world where socks can fly,
Cats converse with the pizza guy,
Flip-flops dance a jolly jig,
While spoons debate if they're too big.

A clock struck twelve, a frog said "Ribbit!"
Chasing shadows, it lost its limit,
Bicycles wear helmets made of cheese,
Ticklish tacos float in the breeze.

In this realm, the cows wear hats,
As turtles chat with friendly bats,
Lemonade rains from cotton clouds,
While laughter forms the merriest crowds.

So let's juggle dreams with glee,
For all that's odd is fair and free,
In frames where logic steps aside,
We skip through worlds with joyful pride.

Phrases in the Ether

Words bounce around like silly springs,
Tickling thoughts, oh what joy it brings,
Worms recite their epic tales,
While jellybeans dress in vibrant veils.

Clouds whisper secrets to the sun,
As squirrels debate who's number one,
Pies perform a waltz in the air,
And grapefruit giggles, quite rare to share.

Lizards play hopscotch on the moon,
While octopuses hum a lively tune,
Turtles wear sunglasses, oh so cool,
Splashing in puddles, defying the rules.

In this dance of nonsensical lines,
Where whispers play in quirky designs,
Let's revel in the absurd delight,
For laughter echoes on this starry night.

Echoes of Time

Tick-tock, says the clock with flair,
As waffles fly through the crisp morning air,
Past and future spin like a top,
With giggles of time, they never stop.

The suitcase started a travel blog,
Documenting adventures with a frog,
Whimsical rides on bacon trains,
While time itself wears silly chains.

A rubber duck gives sage advice,
Dancing upon the stream of rice,
Old mops regale with tales of yore,
As kooky clocks just want to explore.

So let's chase echoes, wildly loud,
Embrace the quirks that make us proud,
For in this space where nonsense reigns,
Time lapses into laughter's veins.

Lyrical Landscapes

In a land of marshmallow trees,
Where the wind sings sweet melodies,
Pizza clouds float in the sky,
As funny fish begin to fly.

Grasshoppers play jazz with delight,
Kites dance around in vibrant flight,
The sun wears shades that spark and shine,
While biscuits brew a cup of fine wine.

Here, owls recite poetry to frogs,
And cats play chess with grumpy dogs,
Balloons giggle with every bounce,
As silly thoughts do quite denounce.

In this whimsical wonderland bright,
Where everything's funny and feels just right,
Let's paint the world with joy and glee,
For laughter's the key to wild jubilee.

Songs of the Spheres

In a galaxy far away,
Planets danced and played all day.
They twirled in a cosmic jest,
Chasing comets as their guest.

Stars giggle, sparkle, and shine,
While black holes pull a funny line.
A gravitational slip and slide,
In the universe, there's no need to hide.

Asteroids often lose their way,
Trying to join the interstellar ballet.
When they bump into a friendly star,
They laugh and go, "That was bizarre!"

The moons make faces, join the fun,
Each orbit a joke, a cosmic pun.
With every eclipse, there's a sigh,
"Look, the sun's peeking; oh my, oh my!"

A Canvas of Cosmic Lines

Constellations sketch a map,
Drawing lines, clap clap clap!
A bear and a hunter chase about,
While some stars just pout and shout.

Nebulae splatter colors bright,
Painting the canvas of the night.
With every swirl and twinkling hue,
The universe laughs, "What's next? How 'bout a shoe?"

Galaxies collide with a smash,
Creating a vibrant, flashy splash.
"Oops! Watch where you're going, friend!"
Echoes through space, with a merry bend.

Black holes are like the cosmic clowns,
Swirling in laughter, upside-down crowns.
In the theater of night, they grin wide,
For in their chaos, joy does abide.

Verses of Variability

In the realm where quirks reside,
Everything seems to take a ride.
One day it's hot, the next it's cold,
Even time has stories to be told.

Astrologers often throw their darts,
At fickle stars with changing hearts.
"Is that a planet or a dream?"
They ponder as they sip their cream.

Lightyears stretch, but jokes are close,
Tickling the cosmos like a ghost.
Relativity winks and takes a bow,
While scientists laugh and say, "Wow!"

So let's toast to the cosmic spree,
Where nothing's quite what it seems to be.
A laugh here, a twist there, oh what a ride,
In the universe's whims, we all abide.

The Language of the Stars

Stars whisper secrets in the night,
In a language that feels just right.
"Did you hear what Mars said today?"
"Went shopping for new rocks, ho hum, hooray!"

Mercury zooms with a cheeky grin,
Racing past while Venus spins.
With every twinkle, there's a chat,
"Uranus smells like a giant cat!"

Saturn's rings are quite the tease,
Swaying gently in a cosmic breeze.
"Catch me if you can," the planets joke,
As they swirl around their celestial cloak.

In the cosmos where laughter reigns,
Aliens burst with joy in refrains.
For even light travels on a giggle,
In a universe where fun is a wiggle.

Cosmic Chorus

In the cosmos, stars do twinkle,
Planets dance and comets crinkle.
A rocket ship with joyful glee,
Sings a tune to a cosmic spree.

Aliens laugh with silly sounds,
While gravity trips and tumbles 'round.
A wormhole swirls, oh what a sight,
It hiccups and giggles in the night.

Shadows and Light

A shadow sly, it skips on by,
Catching a sunbeam in the sky.
It tickles light, it plays a game,
Then hides away, it feels no shame.

When twilight falls, the dance begins,
Stars laugh until the night just spins.
A moonbeam winks with cheeky grace,
And shadows sway, a silly chase.

Waves of Existence

Waves crash down with a bubbly foam,
The ocean sings, it feels like home.
Seagulls squawk in a feathery fight,
As fishy friends swim out of sight.

The tide rolls in, it trips on sand,
With playful glee, the waves expand.
A splashy whale dons a water hat,
While dolphins leap, they say, "How 'bout that?"

The Balance of Being

In a world of topsy-turvy fun,
A juggler spins 'neath the bright sun.
He tosses oranges, catches blue,
And bananas yell, "Look at me too!"

The scale tips left, then swings to right,
Balance beams dance with pure delight.
Life wobbles on a bouncy line,
As laughter rings, it feels divine.

Gravity's Lullaby

In a world where apples fall,
A sleeping moon lets out a call.
Stars giggle in their silver dance,
While comets swirl in cheeky prance.

Planets tease with buoyant flair,
Wobbling in their cosmic air.
Each orbit spins a chuckling tune,
Making black holes chuckle at noon.

Echoes of the Infinite

Whispers bounce on light's bright beam,
Telling tales of a cosmic dream.
Gravity plays with echoes kind,
Bouncing laughter in the blind.

Asteroids sing in playful jest,
Meteors race, they're not at rest.
Galaxies wink with a grin so wide,
In this vastness, we all abide.

Timelines in Dissonance

Time skips like a playful child,
Chasing shadows, always wild.
Past and future, they giggle and jive,
While present moments feel alive.

A clock runs late, it's having fun,
This unkind joke for everyone.
We leap through years, with a silly cheer,
In wobbly loops, we disappear.

Harmonies of the Cosmos

Sing along with starlit bands,
Comets strum with frosty hands.
Jupiter leads in jovial cheer,
While Saturn spins with rings sincere.

Each note, a wink of cosmic fate,
A symphony that won't wait.
Notes collide in vibrant hues,
Making melodies, not just news.

Entangled Moments

In a tangle of thoughts, I trip and I fall,
Time spins around like a dance in a hall.
My coffee's too cold, my donut's too sweet,
Yet life's little quirks make the day feel complete.

A cat in a box, or so they all say,
Is he here or there? Well, who's to display?
My watch plays tricks, it runs fast or slow,
But laughter's the key that makes worries let go.

Ascending Shadows

Shadows climbing high towards the ceiling's bright light,
I stumble and giggle, oh what a sight!
As the sun makes its rounds, the shadows do prance,
In a peculiar game, they have all learned to dance.

Mismatched socks tell tales of a wardrobe gone wild,
Like a kid with a secret, too goofy, too styled.
They wiggle and tease, oh what a delight,
In the world of our shadows, everything's right.

Light's Melodic Path

A beam of bright chatter flits here and then there,
It teases the flowers, just bold enough to dare.
The sun sings a tune that the daisies all hum,
While I try to dance, but just end up a bum.

With giggles of photons darting about,
They play hide and seek, there's no time for doubt.
In the light's joyous jig, I spin and I sway,
Caught in the rhythm, oh what a fine day!

Timeless Triads

Three friends on a bench, sharing laughter and cheer,
They whisper of dreams, and their worries disappear.
With each passing moment, they jest and they play,
In a trio of time, where the hours sway.

Each story they tell, wrapped in giggles and glow,
Builds castles of joy where no shadows can grow.
For when friends entwine in a simple delight,
The essence of time is forever alright.

Melodic Entanglements

In a dance of quarks, they wiggle and spin,
Atoms gossip secrets, where to begin.
With every tick of time, they twist and shout,
Who knew that physics could be this outright?

Waves play hide and seek, a quantum tease,
Light's a gentle jester, always trying to please.
When gravity trips, we all fall down,
Laughing as we float around town!

The Language of Light

Light beams tickle logic, what a sheer delight,
  Conversing in photons, a mystical light.
Einstein cracks jokes while twinkling stars wink,
  Glowing with laughter, what do you think?

Shadows giggle softly, cast by the sun,
  While bending around corners just for fun.
A spectrum of colors in merry array,
  Every hue sings, 'It's a bright kind of day!'

Gravity's Serenade

Gravity pulls like a mother's embrace,
Yet sometimes it trips us, oh what a race!
Falling for laughter, it teases and jests,
In the dance of the cosmos, we all are guests.

The ground says, 'Boo!' with a cheeky grin,
While we try to stand, but just can't win.
With every small bump, the earth seems to cheer,
Gravity's game leaves us giggling in fear!

Stars in Stanzas

Stars scribble wishes in the night sky's guise,
With cosmic ink they play, oh what a surprise!
They rhyme through the ages, in glittering lines,
Comets joining in, making clever designs.

In a cosmic café, the planets convene,
Chatting about orbits, quite the lively scene.
With laughter and light-years, they share a jest,
In this universe, they're truly the best!

Dialogues with Darkness

In shadows where the giggles dwell,
A ghostly jester rings a bell.
He whispers jokes in moonlit night,
And pulls the stars, oh what a sight!

The darkness chuckles, oh so sly,
It tickles dreams as they drift by.
With every shadow, laughter grows,
Even the owls start to doze.

In the corners, secrets scheme,
Twisted plots like a waking dream.
The scary tales take a funny twist,
In the night, who could resist?

So endure the dark with a silly grin,
For laughter's light always wins.
Let's dance with shadows, not in fright,
And turn the spooky into light.

The Rhythm of Existence

Life taps out a funky beat,
With hiccups and claps from happy feet.
A dance-off with the setting sun,
Is this existence? Oh, so fun!

The timekeeper's got two left feet,
His clockwork speaks in silly tweets.
Every tick has a bouncing rhyme,
In this waltz through the sands of time.

Galaxies spin, but what a show,
With comets zigzagging to and fro.
The planets giggle and twirl around,
In the vastness, joy is found.

So let's cha-cha through the days,
In this wacky cosmic maze.
Embrace the rhythm, take a twirl,
Life's just a dance, give it a whirl!

Verses Between Realms

Two realms collided in a laugh,
One's a wizard, the other, a calf.
They swap their hats and share a quirk,
Mixing magic with a smelly jerk.

In the field of cotton candy dreams,
Where everyone giggles and nothing seems.
A dragon plays hopscotch with a mouse,
Building castles in a tinfoil house.

The clouds are pink with jelly beans,
And grass is green in polka dot jeans.
Frogs sing symphonies to dancing flies,
Underneath the glittering skies.

Such verses play in silly tones,
In this land, no one moans.
Join the laughter, take a leap,
In realms where nonsense runs deep.

Tapestry of Time

Threads of moments, woven in glee,
Stitched with laughter, wild and free.
Chronicles of giggles, soft and bright,
A patchwork quilt of day and night.

Each tick a treasure, each tock a tune,
A snail races 'neath the light of the moon.
With yarns of hilarity, let's create,
A comedy show of fate and weight.

In this fabric, colors collide,
Old socks and shoelaces side by side.
Hiccups of time, they twist and twirl,
In our tapestry, watch it unfurl.

So pull a thread, let's weave a rhyme,
In this crafty dance of time.
With every stitch, laughter's the key,
In this quilted land, we are all free.

Quantum Stanzas

In a world where cats can fly,
Chasing mice in the sky.
Atoms jiggle, do a dance,
A quantum leap, a wild chance.

Time is stretchy, like a string,
Bouncing back, it makes you sing.
I lost my watch, but who needs time?
Let's float in space, it feels so prime.

A particle goes zooming by,
Waving hello as it flies high.
You ask it 'What's the rush today?'
It giggles back, 'Just on my way!'

Space is filled with giggles, too,
Planets wink in shades of blue.
Gravity's just a silly trick,
Pulling at us, quite comedic!

Syllables of Spacetime

Wibbly wobbly words collide,
In this verse, let laughter ride.
Gravity holds a giant clown,
Falling slowly, but never frown.

Einstein whispers jokes in rhyme,
Proving laughter bends all time.
A spinning top begins to sway,
Laughing at its dizzy day.

Black holes hiding silly things,
Lost socks, and capes with magic wings.
They burp and laugh, a cosmic show,
Where humor travels fast, you know.

Dancing dots in neon hue,
Paint the night with giggles too.
Silly quarks in fun parade,
In a universe where jokes are made!

Celestial Verses

Stars twinkle like a cheeky grin,
Planets roll in a cosmic din.
Meteor showers make a splash,
Falling stars make wishes, oh what a dash.

In the void, a comet teases,
Tickling us with cosmic breezes.
Galaxies braid like hair gone wild,
A universe where jokes are compiled.

Shooting beams of light, they play,
In this vast reach, come what may.
Asteroids dance in a merry line,
Creating laughter through space and time.

Supernovas burst with glee,
Exploding into confetti, whee!
In a whimsical cosmic play,
We laugh and spin the night away.

Threads of the Universe

Tangled threads of cosmic fate,
Weaving stories that twist and sate.
A string pulls tight, then it lets go,
In this fun game, we laugh and flow.

Light years giggle as they race,
Comets chase with happy face.
In a tapestry of jests and puns,
We dance along till day is done.

Quarks are jumping in a band,
Forming laughter, oh so grand.
Time skips like a playful child,
In a universe so wily and wild.

With a wink and a playful shove,
The cosmos whispers tales of love.
So let's embrace this humor spree,
In the threads of space, wild and free!

Notes from the Nebula

In a cloud of gas and dust,
Spaceships find a way to rust.
Aliens giggle, oh what a sight,
Chasing comets in the night.

Stars throw parties, lights go boom,
Planets swipe in the cosmic room.
One dances left, the other right,
They trip on moons, what a funny flight!

Galactic pranks, they pull with glee,
Asteroids bounce like they're on spree.
Black holes laugh, they swirl with pride,
"Try not to fall in!" they must chide.

Every twinkle holds a jest,
In this universe, we're just a guest.
With each giggle, stars do spin,
Holding secrets from within.

Voices of the Void

In the silence, a voice does shout,
"Did you hear that? What's it about?"
Echoes chuckle, stars play along,
Making music, a cosmic song.

Nebulas hum their silly tunes,
Twinkling brightly, beneath the moons.
"Is that Mars wearing my hat?"
"Oh, surely not, just a funky brat!"

Galaxies spin in a joyful whirl,
As comets frolic and do a twirl.
Planets gossip, "What's up with Earth?"
"Always so serious, what's that worth?"

In this emptiness, laughter thrives,
Creating humor, it truly strives.
So when you gaze at the night's embrace,
Know that laughter fills this space.

Chronicles of Cosmic Dancers

In a ball of stars, they swirl and sway,
Dancing comets keep the beat at bay.
Galaxy girls in sequined lights,
Twirl and tease the satellite nights.

Supernovae burst, a grand debut,
"Watch me shine!" they say, "Look at my hue!"
Black holes laugh, they pull in the show,
"For a quick spin; let's go with the flow!"

Planets form a conga line,
Bumping together, feeling fine.
Meteor showers rain down confetti,
"Is this a party? Oh, I'm so ready!"

With each twirl, the universe beams,
Joking cosmos pull at our dreams.
So raise your glass to the stars so bright,
For in their dance, we find delight.

The Fluidity of Form

Time warps here, bends and sways,
A wrinkled pancake in crazy ways.
Einstein giggles, "What's a line?"
"Let's curve it, make it all align!"

Space suits shape like wiggly jell,
Navigators can't tell their bell.
In a wormhole, they slip and slide,
"Haven't laughed this hard; enjoy the ride!"

Matter floats, like thoughts in air,
Silly shapes showing off with flair.
"Look! A triangle just did a flip!"
"Oh dear, I think I'll lose my grip!"

From a quark to galaxy wide,
All forms giggle, no need to hide.
In this twisted space-time frame,
You'll find the cosmos loves the game.

Enigmas of Existence

In a world where socks go on the run,
And cats plot under the guise of fun.
The toaster pops bread with a sassy flip,
While spoons conspire on a secret trip.

Time ticks backward on a lazy noon,
While clouds chase the moon in a balloon.
Laughter echoes from a rubber plant,
As squirrels negotiate with the distant ant.

A sandwich talks about its filling plight,
While chairs debate the best way to sit tight.
The fridge hums tunes of lost leftovers,
While calendars plot their own takeovers.

In this dance of jumbled sense,
We find joy in every pretense.
For what's existence if not a jest?
A riddle we live, in chaos, our quest.

The Music of Mist

In the morning, mist does a little jig,
While trees play tag with a peppy twig.
The sun wears shades, all cool and bright,
While shadows sneak in for a game of fright.

Whispers float in the air so thick,
As raindrops giggle, a merry trick.
Each breeze hums a tune, soft and sly,
While birds join in from the nearby sky.

The puddles dance with a watery grace,
And frogs leap high in a funky race.
It's a jam session under the dew,
Where the world spins tales of the silly and true.

In the hush of dawn, where secrets persist,
We laugh with the chaos, the humor, the twist.
For in this sweet fog, we find reason to sing,
As nature composes its own wild fling.

Reflections in the Resonance

In a puddle, I see my doppelgänger frown,
While umbrellas try to wear a crown.
A mirror lies, claiming to be wise,
As I dodge raindrops and dance with surprise.

Echoes bounce like a bouncy ball,
While speakers whisper secrets to the hall.
The clock ticks loud, though time's in a daze,
As chairs spin tales in their creaky ways.

Through the looking glass, reality sways,
As oranges ponder their bright display.
In this playful realm where nonsense is king,
We chase after shadows that giggle and sing.

With every beat, the world seems to bend,
As laughter and logic do twist and blend.
For in these reflections of silly intent,
We find the joy in each moment spent.

Harmony Beyond Horizons

In a world where socks don't match,
Cats ride bicycles, and time's a catch.
Juggling planets, oh what a twist,
Gravity's laughter we can't resist.

Einstein's hair in a wild fro,
Tick-tock, tick-tock, but where'd time go?
Bananas play tunes on the moonlight stage,
While fish wear hats, flipping the page.

Cups of tea in the stars we sip,
Dancing on clouds, what a quirky trip!
Zebras in stripes run a wacky race,
As jellybeans bounce in this funny space.

Lemurs twist in a comical plight,
Crickets recite in the dead of night.
Each giggle echoes in a cosmic hall,
Where fun and laughter unite us all.

Polyrhythms of Existence

A squirrel beats drums on a rusty pipe,
While frogs moonwalk, oh what a hype!
Dancing through realms of giggles and glee,
To the sound of a cat who sings off-key.

Stars are busy polishing their shoes,
While comets exchange their funniest news.
Jellyfish waltz in a sparkling sea,
With octopuses strumming a melody.

Time rolls its eyes at the jester's show,
As clocks ring bells that nobody knows.
Raindrops tap dance on windowpanes,
In this wacky place where logic refrains.

Giraffes play chess with the clouds up high,
While pancakes flip and take to the sky.
Each giggling moment is one we embrace,
In this cosmic jam of a funny space.

Celestial Cadences

Aliens bake cookies on Saturn rings,
Under the watch of three-headed kings.
With chocolate comets and sprinkles of stars,
They giggle and flip through interstellar bars.

Galaxies spin like tops on a floor,
While unicorns dance, never a bore.
Planets play tag, dodging cosmic cars,
In a nebula buzzing with laughter and jars.

Time takes a tumble, with joy it rolls,
Wormholes provide the punchline goals.
Each joke travels faster than light can chase,
In this whimsical, tangle-free space.

Nebulas puff with a comedic flair,
As laughter erupts from everywhere.
Join the fun, come take a spin,
In this galaxy circus, let the giggles begin!

Whispers in Warp

Bubbles of laughter float through the void,
Where spacetime twists and time is toyed.
Whirling about with a wink and a nudge,
Comets collide with a giggling grudge.

Black holes play peek-a-boo with delight,
As photons dance, twinkling bright.
Chasing the echoes of a cosmic tune,
With jellyfish gliding past the pale moon.

Curly-tailed time-traveling hounds,
Chasing their tails through odd looping rounds.
Each woof creates a ripple of cheer,
In a universe giggling through space and sphere.

Stars whisper secrets of comical tales,
As aliens gossip with colorful sails.
In this warp where nonsense unfurls,
Laughter bursts forth, interstellar whirls!

Cosmic Echoes

In a galaxy far, far away,
A cow jumps over a comet's play.
Stars giggle and twinkle, so bright,
While black holes munch on snacks at night.

Planets dance in their own groove,
With asteroids doing the cosmic move.
Jupiter spins in polka dot glee,
While Mercury steals his cookie, oh me!

Uranus grins, it's quite a sight,
As Saturn dons rings, oh so tight!
The universe chuckles, keeps on whirling,
With every oddity, it keeps unfurling.

In this wacky space-bound affair,
Smile at the quirks we all must share.
For in this cosmos, strange and vast,
Every laugh echoes and will forever last.

Celestial Whispers

Planets whisper secrets, oh so sly,
The Sun winks, saying 'Oh me, oh my!'
Venus giggles, a beauty with flair,
While Mars jokes, 'Who's got time to spare?'

Comets zoom by with tails of light,
Making wishes on a starry night.
Neptune chuckles, it's quite humorous,
Saying, 'My color? I'm notorious!'

Asteroids play tag, round and round,
While moons hum tunes, a soft, sweet sound.
A cosmic joke shared through the stars,
Making us laugh, no need for bars.

So lift your gaze, let laughter fly,
At the jokes whispered in the night sky.
For in the cosmos, we all find cheer,
As celestial giggles are always near.

Time's Tapestry

Time weaves a quilt, patch by patch,
Each piece a memory, a lovey-dovey batch.
Chronos tickles the seconds that flee,
While minutes rendezvous for tea.

Yesterday's sock got lost in the fray,
While tomorrows chase, just a milky way.
Hours play hopscotch, doing their dance,
As future laughs at the past's lost chance.

Tick-tock sings in a comical way,
Each chime a note in the grand ballet.
As calendars pirouette through the air,
Time's tapestry stitches without a care.

So let's embrace this whimsical flow,
For in each second, surprises will grow.
In a world that spins silly and fleet,
Every tick brings laughter—what a treat!

Gravity's Lullaby

Gravity hums a sweet little tune,
As it tugs on the moon like a sly raccoon.
Stars hang around, just swaying in place,
While comets curse at their clumsy race.

'Hey there, Earth, don't take my cheese!'
Cried the troublesome moon, up in the breeze.
The sun just laughed, oh what a jest,
While planets rock-a-bye, doing their best.

In this dance of hold and sway,
Nothing's too heavy, just floating away.
So let's launch jokes up to the sky,
With gravity's grip, we'll never say bye!

So close your eyes, let laughter creep,
As gravity sings us all into sleep.
When morning comes, joy will arise,
Bouncing like bunnies under brightening skies.

Infinite Dance

In a cosmic hall where stars prance,
Gravity's tune leads the fun dance.
Galaxies twirl, a sight to see,
Even black holes join with glee.

Planets spin in a merry whirl,
In the milky way, watch them twirl.
Comets laugh as they zoom right by,
While asteroids waltz through the sky.

Celestial bodies, in frolicking flight,
Chasing each other, oh what a sight.
Meteor showers, like confetti fall,
In this great ball, they invite us all.

So let's grab a partner and spin with flair,
Round and round without a care.
In this infinite ballroom, we prance and sway,
Forever dancing, come what may.

Paradox of Light

A photon's journey takes quite a ride,
Faster than thought, it won't even hide.
It jumps through space, with a wink and a grin,
While waiting for light, we just might win.

In the theater of time, it plays hide and seek,
Flickering bright, yet always so weak.
It travels in waves, a nifty little trick,
A paradox making the wise go quick.

When clocks start ticking, it races away,
Yet here we stand, still making the play.
In mirrors it dances, reflecting delight,
A puzzling performance, this paradox of light.

So grab your sunglasses, the show is on,
A cosmic comedy, from dusk till dawn.
Join the giggle as we ponder and muse,
The speed of our beams is the best type of ruse.

Echoes in the Void

In the vast dark, where silence hums,
Echoes frolic, like quirky chums.
They bounce off stars, in a jovial jest,
Making whispers that never take rest.

"Hello!" shouts one, with a cheeky grin,
While others reply, "Come join in!"
They play tag with waves, all light and sound,
In the emptiness, laughter is found.

A cosmic chorus, a cosmic cheer,
With no one around, it's perfectly clear.
They dance and they dive in the emptiness wild,
In the void they frolic, like a mischievous child.

So next time you're star-gazing alone,
Listen for giggles from the great unknown.
For echoes are pranking, just out of sight,
In the quiet abyss, they spread pure delight.

Celestial Symphonies

In the cosmos, an orchestra plays,
With planets and moons in a musical haze.
Each note is a star, twinkling bright,
Creating a melody, pure delight.

The sun strums chords, while comets flit,
Each passing meteor adds to the wit.
While black holes hum, with gravity's sigh,
In this grand concert, we dream to fly.

This symphony swirls, through spaces unseen,
With rhythm and laughter, oh so serene.
Galaxies gather for the ultimate show,
As celestial sounds stair-step from low.

So raise your hands, let's dance to the beat,
In this cosmic gathering, joyous and sweet.
For in the universe, music lasts long,
In celestial symphonies, we all belong.

Threads of Infinity

In a world where thoughts can soar,
Ideas bounce off every door.
Laughter stretches through the air,
As we find giggles everywhere.

Time's a jigsaw, pieces askew,
Fitting nonsense in with the true.
With every twist, a pun emerges,
And in the chaos, mirth diverges.

We dance through loops of endless days,
Lost in spirals, we find our ways.
Grinning at what we can't control,
The jokes keep rolling, that's the goal.

So twirl your thoughts, and let them roam,
In this universe, we call home.
With quips and laughs, we intertwine,
Creating wonders, oh so divine.

Constellations in Verse

Stars are winking in the night,
With tales of love, and silly fright.
Each twinkle shares a secret joke,
In the cosmos, funny dreams invoke.

Galaxies spin like tops in play,
Comets racing, laughing away.
Astroids bump with a silly sound,
In this dance, joy is always found.

Planets swirl in clownish glee,
With every orbit, they skip with glee.
Gravity pulls, but we float high,
Chasing smiles across the sky.

So join the dance, let's take a chance,
In the universe, let's laugh and prance.
With every verse, we lose the gloom,
In spiral arms, find joy to bloom.

The Tale of Time

Tick-tock goes the silly clock,
In this tale, let's take stock.
Time on roller skates, you see,
Races by, just like a bee.

Seconds giggle, minutes tease,
"Catch us if you can!" they squeeze.
Hours juggle, twisting round,
In this circus, laughs abound.

Days in costumes, waving wide,
Play silly games, and let us slide.
Time's a clown, with tricks on hand,
Turning moments into sand.

So let's not worry, just have fun,
In this tapestry, everyone's a pun.
With each tick, giggles we'll find,
In this tale of time, let's unwind.

Melodies of Maybes

Whimsical notes drift in the air,
With every tune, we dance with flair.
Melodies wrapping us like a hug,
Humming with joy, we're still a bug.

What if notes all chose to chat?
Would we find the meaning in that?
Or would jokes play on repeat,
With rhythms fast, and shuffles sweet?

Maybe this song is just a tease,
Inviting laughter with perfect ease.
Every beat, a twist we explore,
In cheerful tunes, we want more.

So let the melodies intertwine,
As we sing our way through the line.
With maybes swirling around our head,
In perfect harmony, joy is spread.

Tempo of Tranquility

In the garden where time bends,
Butterflies giggle, making amends.
Squirrels debate on the best way to leap,
While I sip lemonade, drifting to sleep.

Clouds race by in a game of tag,
A snail climbs high, gives time a brag.
Chasing shadows, we tickle the sun,
Joy in the chaos, oh what fun!

The clock's lost its nerve, can't find its beat,
As laughter dances on cartoonish feet.
In this realm where silly reigns supreme,
Life's a waltz in a whimsical dream.

So let's sway to the rhythm of cheer,
With giggles that linger, bring friends near.
In the tempo of goofiness, sing loud,
For in this moment, we're all quite proud.

Weightless Words

Floating on phrases, high in the air,
Witty banter flows without a care.
Each laugh is a feather, light as a kite,
Twisting metaphors, soaring with delight.

Gobbling up puns like candy on a spree,
Whispers of humor carry us, you see.
We fashion a chorus of tickles and glee,
In a world where gravity's lost its decree.

Nonsense and giggles, a card up our sleeve,
Juggling our thoughts, we can hardly believe.
With quips that unravel like soft, silly strings,
We laugh at the chaos that each moment brings.

So buoyant, we bounce from one joke to the next,
In this flight of fancy, the world is perplexed.
With charmingly wild, weightless good cheer,
Let's tether our joy, for laughter's near!

Cadence in Chaos

In the jumble of life, we dance askew,
With rhythm so quirky, it's joy that we brew.
Puppies and kittens, they prance on the floor,
While socks go missing, lost in folklore.

The blender's a drummer, with beats out of line,
As coffee spills over, a caffeinated sign.
We twirl in a waltz with the dust bunnies near,
And each accidental slip births a cheer.

An orchestra of clatter, a symphony bright,
Where laughter and chaos perform every night.
With clocks that melt down, we gather our crew,
To celebrate nonsense in all that we do.

So embrace quirks, let your spirit rise,
In this lively cacophony, joy multiplies.
For in chaos, we find a harmonious flow,
With the rhythm of fun, let good times grow!

Verses in the Vortex

In a whirlpool of words, we take a grand spin,
Round and round, where does the fun begin?
An octopus juggling, it throws us a wink,
While we're busy tumbling, not stopping to think.

With giggles like bubbles, we float to the top,
In the twinkling vortex, we swirl, never stop.
An umbrella's a hat, in this playful storm,
And every new twist keeps the laughter warm.

Marshmallows bouncing in gravity's dance,
With flying balloons, we take every chance.
In the center of mayhem, we're free as a kite,
Where nonsense runs riot, and everything's bright.

So spin with abandon through verses absurd,
Each twist, every turn, a delightful word.
In the vortex of joy, let our spirits ignite,
For life's just a giggle when shared with delight!

The Rhythm of Space

In the cosmos, stars do twirl,
Dancing with a planetary swirl.
Galaxies giggle in their play,
While comets race and veer away.

Asteroids toss like balls at night,
While Saturn's rings shine so bright.
Black holes laugh with their big grin,
Swallowing light with a gleeful spin.

Space dust chuckles, a playful tease,
Tickling planets with a cosmic breeze.
Every quark's a joker, all in jest,
Winking at the universe's best.

So let's join in this stellar fling,
With moonbeams laughing and stars that sing.
In this grand cosmic hullabaloo,
Let's dance like galaxies, me and you.

Celestial Choreography

The sun winks at the moon's shy grin,
While planets spin like a disco pin.
Neptune twirls in a watery pirouette,
Uranus giggles, the oddest duet.

Mars throws a party, it's red, it's loud,
With little moons bouncing, oh, so proud!
Jupiter's storm is the punchline here,
While satirical rings ring in cheer.

Shooting stars make wishes and pop,
Eclipses have jokes that never stop.
Stars gather round for a comedy roast,
In the great dark space, they laugh the most.

So come to this dance emceed by light,
With laughter that echoes throughout the night.
In the vast, endless giggle of sky,
We'll step on the cosmos, you and I.

Whirlwinds of Time

Tick tock, tick tock, the clock's got flair,
Time does the tango, swirling through air.
Past and future, a dizzying spin,
One moment's loss, another win.

Seconds race with a zany leap,
While minutes chuckle, secret they're keeping.
Hours in hats, the silliest sight,
Twirling around under the moonlight.

"To be or not to be," the ages quote,
As bygone eras dance on their boat.
Every tick is a joke to share,
With whimsical moments beyond compare.

So embrace the whirl, the slip, the slide,
In the vortex of time, let's take a ride.
With laughter echoing in every chime,
We'll find the fun in the whirlwinds of time.

Interstellar Serenade

In the midnight sky, where silence reigns,
A tune of stardust lightly gains.
The planets hum a catchy beat,
While meteors make it sound so sweet.

Singing bright as a comet flies,
With laughter bubbling like moonlit skies.
Pulsars thump like a cosmic drum,
In the vastness, we're never glum.

Alien jokes from far-off lands,
Are shared in whispers by tiny hands.
Each galactic note, a joyful spark,
Lighting up the universe's dark.

So gather 'round, let the tunes unfurl,
With a universal jig, let's dance and swirl.
In this interstellar, laughing parade,
We'll sing together, unafraid.

Pulses of the Cosmos

When stars dance out in cosmic glee,
They giggle in a gravity-free spree.
Planets wobble with silly spins,
Creating laughter from where it begins.

A comet jests as it zooms past,
Tickling the moons, oh what a blast!
Galaxies swirl in a twinkling show,
As light-years tickle, up high they glow.

Asteroids chuckle, bouncing around,
Making mischief without a sound.
In this universe, absurd and wide,
Laughter echoes, a cosmic tide.

The sun winks down with a radiant grin,
The vastness of space is where we begin.
Playful pulses in every direction,
Creating joy in sweet connection.

Infinity in Meter

In realms where time does silly hops,
Counting seconds just never stops.
Each tickle of a clock bends wonky truth,
Infinity laughs, what's age to youth?

Eons flip like a pancake stack,
One minute's here, the next is whack!
Measuring moments with a rubber band,
Stretching time till it can't quite stand.

Dancing digits in a never-ending race,
In this meter, we're lost in space.
So let's twirl with seconds and sing with glee,
For in this measure, we're truly free!

With silly sums, we'll round and round,
Eternity trips on forgetful ground.
In numbers' antics, a giggle's found,
Infinite laughter without a bound.

Orbits of Emotion

In love's orbit, we spin and sway,
With laughter mixed in the fun of play.
Hearts do the tango, twirl around,
In every circle, pure joy is found.

Friendship's planets, in orbits they glide,
Bumping and giggling side by side.
Sadness takes a silly turn,
In this dance, bright flames still burn.

Jokes fly high on emotional swings,
Creating moments, oh the joy it brings!
As we twirl through troubles and delight,
In orbit's embrace, we laugh at night.

Every feeling spins, what a show,
Round and round, come join the flow.
With each burst of laughter, we shall see,
Emotional orbits set us free.

Patterns of the Celestial

Stars etch patterns on cosmic sheets,
While squishy meteors dance to funky beats.
In the tapestry of night, they play,
Creating shapes that sway and sway.

Constellations giggle, what a sight!
Drawing silly lines in the velvet night.
Circles, triangles, and zigzag lore,
Patterns of joy we can't ignore.

The moon wears stripes with a cheeky grin,
As clouds in pajamas spin and spin.
Each formation tells a story so bright,
Crafted in laughter, wrapped in light.

In this celestial dance, we all take part,
With quirky sketches that warm the heart.
Patterns of fun in the skies above,
Whispering secrets of laughter and love.

Fractured Time

In a clock that spins the wrong way,
Minutes giggle and play stray.
Days wear hats made of cheese,
While seconds dance with the breeze.

Yesterday's socks found in today,
Waltzing along in disarray.
Time gets dizzy, starts to laugh,
When we try to split it in half.

Tick-tock becomes a silly song,
Where hours argue who's right or wrong.
Seconds slip through a silly maze,
Leaving us lost in a daze.

When time runs off to take a break,
It leaves us wondering what's at stake.
In a world where clocks lose their mind,
We find laughs that are one of a kind.

Quantum Heartbeats

In a universe small and neat,
Particles dance with little feet.
They wave and smile, quite a sight,
Twirling joyfully, day and night.

Each heartbeat's a cosmic chance,
Swaying wildly in a quantum dance.
You blink, they're here, you blink, they're gone,
Always teasing, just beyond.

A cat is both here and not,
In a box, it plays the jokester's plot.
Laughs echo in a superposition,
Whiskered giggles in a strange condition.

When love's entangled, hearts collide,
In a string of laughter, we'll abide.
Though separated by space and time,
Joy remains the universal rhyme.

Starlit Connections

Stars giggle across the night,
Winking down, oh what a sight.
Constellations play hide and seek,
Turning bright, then feeling meek.

Planets chat with silly glee,
Muttering secrets just for me.
Comets laugh as they zoom past,
Leaving trails of sparkles fast.

A galaxy spins in playful might,
While black holes munch on starlit light.
In this cosmic playground, we find,
Connections dancing, undefined.

Each twinkle holds a story clear,
Galactic giggles we all hear.
In the vastness, we unite,
With starlit smiles shining bright.

Orbital Musings

In a whirl of planets making rounds,
Gravity leaps in silly bounds.
Falling stars start a crazy spree,
While moons just laugh in harmony.

Kites of comets soar so high,
Snaring dreams that float by.
As orbits twist like rubber bands,
In this dance, no one understands.

Rockets take a goofy dive,
Chasing giggles, feeling alive.
Asteroids stumble past to say,
"We're just here for the play!"

So let's embrace the cosmic cheer,
Via the galaxies, far and near.
In this whirl of fun out there,
We find a laugh in the cosmic air.

Melodies of the Multiverse

In a universe vast, with tunes that can dance,
Every note is a chance, oh what a romance!
A cat sings a tune while it's chasing a mouse,
In a world filled with laughter, we all fit this house.

Planets sway gently on cosmic marionette strings,
While asteroids play tag, oh the joy that it brings!
A comet zips by, with a wink and a grin,
In this symphony crazy, let the fun begin!

Stars burst like popcorn in a celestial pot,
Galaxies giggle, oh, they like to joke a lot!
With every cosmic flip, there's still room for jest,
In this ball of existence, who could love it less?

So gather your friends in this space-faring craft,
Through laughter and music, we'll all take a laugh!
In the multiverse's waltz, let's swirl with delight,
As the melodies echo through the stars every night.

Fractals of Fate

In a world that expands like a funny balloon,
Every twist and each turn is a wacky cartoon.
With branches like fingers, fate takes a leap,
Gardens of chaos, where time takes a steep.

The future's a jigsaw of kooky designs,
Each piece brings a chuckle, oh how it shines!
Engines of laughter, on destiny's wheels,
We roll down the hill as the fate spiral peels.

Snowflakes are fractals of whimsical cheer,
Each one a reminder, keep wonder near!
In the maze of existence, we play hide and seek,
While the cosmos chuckles, all fabulous and sleek.

So dance with the chaos, give destiny a twirl,
In the fractals of fate, let your laughter unfurl!
Embrace the absurd, it's where joy resonates,
In designs of the universe, we navigate fates.

The Dance of Dimensions

In a room full of doors that all lead to surprise,
Dimensions take turns in curious disguise.
One twirls on a sofa, another on a chair,
While a third tries to balance on the edge of air.

A wormhole can wiggle with a shimmy and shake,
While time takes a break for a chocolate cake.
We laugh at the oddities that place us in sync,
In this dance of dimensions, we bubble and blink.

Light zips through the fabric, taut as can be,
As shadows play games, how silly they see!
Each leap into laughter, so wild and so free,
In this party of space, we're all meant to be.

So let's cha-cha through realities, twist and shout,
In this fantastic dance, there's no doubt!
With each cosmic jiggle, our spirits will soar,
As the dance of dimensions leaves us wanting more!

Beyond the Horizon

Where the sun meets the moon in a silly charade,
Beyond the horizon, all worries do fade.
Pigs fly with umbrellas, and clouds wear a hat,
When horizons are funny, life's too grand for a spat.

The waves play peek-a-boo with the shores as they laugh,

While mountains join in for a ticklish gaffe.
Each sunset a canvas of giggles and cheer,
Painting horizons where fun is held dear.

Stars twinkle with mischief, a spark in each eye,
Whispering secrets of silliness high.
In the land of the whimsical, life's a grand quest,
Beyond the horizon, we're truly at our best.

So venture with glee, let your spirit take flight,
Beyond every horizon, find pure delight!
In the universe wide, where laughter's the key,
Let's chase after joy, wild and fancy-free!

The Symphony of Stars

In the night sky, stars dance with glee,
They play a tune, wild and free.
A comet sneezes, makes a bright flare,
While planets gossip without a care.

Mars told Venus a joke so old,
Saturn chuckled, its rings uncontrolled.
A black hole yawned, it's time for a snack,
It sucked in laughter, but never looked back.

Galaxies whirl, like a cosmic show,
With shooting stars putting on a flow.
Twinkling stars sing, in tones quite bizarre,
They joke: "How did we get this far?"

The universe giggles at its own grand scheme,
As comets wink at every dream.
In this strange space, where time bends art,
The funny floats inside every heart.

Parallels in Poetry

Lines that run parallel, yet never meet,
Write a sonnet, but it's still offbeat.
Limericks tangle in their quirky rhyme,
While whispers of galaxies roam through time.

One verse declares, "Life's just a game,"
While another says, "It's all the same."
The punchline of laughter is tucked in the verse,
Where words play hide-and-seek, oh, what a curse!

Quasars snicker with poetic flair,
While metaphors float like cosmic air.
Each stanza a journey, a laugh in the void,
With puns and humor, our minds are employed.

In shadows of stardust, our verses collide,
While rhythms of nonsense take us for a ride.
With ink from the cosmos, let the fun stay,
In the realm of the silly, we'll find our way.

Cosmic Connections

Twinkling stars send messages bright,
Like cosmic emails, oh what a sight!
A wormhole opens, it's laugh out loud,
With jokes from the universe, it gathers a crowd.

"Why did the nebula refuse to dance?"
"It said it had no stars for romance!"
Asteroids giggle, on a wild chase,
As meteors race in a comical race.

Black holes take selfies, but they're never clear,
While pulsars tick-tock, year after year.
Time bends and twists in a comical guise,
As laughter echoes through cosmic skies.

In this grand scheme, with humor's embrace,
Connections of planets, they share a space.
So join the dance in the stellar delight,
Where laughter is timeless, and jokes take flight.

Ephemeral Echoes

In the vast universe, echoes can play,
They bounce off nebulae in a quirky way.
"Did you hear that?" the stars often jest,
As black holes chuckle, "We love a good fest!"

The echoes of laughter ripple through night,
As comets wink while taking flight.
A supernova sneezes, bursts with a grin,
And all of creation joins in on the din.

Each fleeting moment, a ticklish delight,
In the cosmic joke, we find our light.
Galactic giggles in the fabric of time,
Where humor and stardust forever will chime.

So dance with the echoes, don't miss out the fun,
In the universe's laughter, we're never done.
For in every twinkle, a moment we share,
With cosmic reflections that tickle the air.

The Pulse of the Universe

In the cosmos so wide, we spin and we sway,
Stars dance with delight, in a quirky ballet.
Planets roll round like a game of charades,
Tickling each other, with comet cascades.

Galaxies giggle, colliding in glee,
A cosmic sitcom, just you wait and see.
Asteroids chuckle as they whiz right by,
Trying to catch a shooting star in the sky.

Saturn wears rings, but thinks they're a hat,
While Jupiter bounces, a jovial brat.
Light-years of laughter ripple through space,
Making the cosmos a jolly old place.

So let's raise a toast to the whims of the night,
In this wacky universe, everything's light.
With a wink and a twinkle, it all comes alive,
In this laughter-filled dance where the dwellers survive.

Time's Tenuous Tune

Oh time is a trickster, it hops and it jumps,
Sometimes it lingers and sometimes it thumps.
Minutes get lost, like socks in a wash,
And seconds play tag, with a cheeky little posh.

Clocks tick and tock with a rhythm absurd,
As if they're all part of a sneaky old bird.
Tickles from seconds that vanish too soon,
Leave us all wondering, where's the next noon?

Time squabbles lightly, with hours at bay,
A jester in chaos, making fun of our play.
Days laugh out loud as they twist and they curl,
In the hey-day of moments that twirl and unfurl.

So next time you fret over a second or two,
Remember the dance, and just join in the hue.
Turn up the volume, and let the fun bloom,
For all of the moments are filling the room.

Ballad of the Boundless

In a world without end, where the wacky winds blow,
The mind takes a trip, with each thought in tow.
Mountains of nonsense and valleys of jest,
Make the journey delightful, a curious quest.

Ideas collide like bubbles in air,
Bouncing and bursting without a care.
Thoughts leap like frogs from lily to pad,
Each splash of creation makes giggles we've had.

Imagination's engine runs wild and untamed,
Chasing after dreams with a laugh that's inflamed.
Boundless as laughter, it swirls on the breeze,
Teasing the thinkers with whims that appease.

So let's cozy up to this funny frontier,
With a chuckle and grin, let's explore without fear.
For in this vast canvas of utter delight,
The ballad keeps playing, through day and through night.

Songs of the Singularity

In the realm where the layers of worlds intertwine,
Rhythms of chaos make everything shine.
Waves of the oddity swirl all around,
Tickling the senses, with giggles abound.

A pixel a hop, a byte with a cheer,
The singularity hums, full of mischief and leer.
With each quirky quark that bounces about,
Creating a chorus that dances with clout.

Silly dimensions, they jump and they prance,
As time does a tango, inviting the chance.
Every twist and twirl sparks laughter's delight,
In the songs of the cosmos, we're ready to flight.

So let's sing together, in harmony's rhyme,
Join hands with the quirky, lose track of the time.
In this joyous playground of infinite fun,
The songs of the singularity have just begun!

Spirals of Existence

In circles we go, like a dizzying dance,
Chasing our tails, in a comical trance.
The dog thinks it's fun, but I just feel weird,
Spiraling round, like a top that's been steered.

Each twist and turn, a giggle escapes,
Like cats in a box, or clumsy shapes.
Life's spinning plates, balancing cheer,
Gravity's joke, only we can't hear.

Harmonies of the Unknown

Singing with aliens, who can't quite hum,
Every note off-key, what a funny strum!
They clap with eight hands, I'm in awe yet amused,
In this cosmic choir, I feel so confused.

The stars wink back, as we tune in and out,
Creating a tune, of laughter and doubt.
Harmony's lost in the great cosmic show,
As space ticks the time, in a wibbly glow.

Dimensions of Dream

In a realm where socks vanish, lost in the fray,
I trip over landscapes, where shadows play.
Floating on marshmallows, clouds made of cream,
Life's playful puzzle, absurd as a dream.

I met a great dragon, who cooked me a pie,
With ingredients strange, like a wink from the sky.
In these silly dimensions, delightfully spun,
It's a world where logic just runs out of fun.

The Gravity within Us

We bounce like balloons, with giggles galore,
Opposites attract, so I just can't ignore.
Your jokes pull me closer, a magnetic force,
While we float through the laughter, on a playful course.

Like grapes in a blender, who swirls the best?
Our lives collide, a cosmic jest.
With a wink and a nod, we'll conquer the fuss,
For silly's the secret, the gravity in us.

www.ingramcontent.com/pod-product-compliance
Lightning Source LLC
Chambersburg PA
CBHW051656160426
43209CB00004B/924